Tales from Toddler Hell

▲·■·▲·■·▲·■·▲·■·▲·■·▲·■·▲·■·▲·■·▲·■·▲·■

Tales from Toddler Hell

▲·■·▲·■·▲

My Life

As a Mom

▲·■·▲·■·▲

Joan Leonard

PHAROS BOOKS
NEW YORK

Some of the essays included here have been published previously in *Parents* magazine and in *The New York Times*.

Jacket design by Douglas & Voss Group
Book design by Suzanne Reisel

LIBRARY OF CONGRESS CATALOGING-IN-PUBLICATION DATA
Leonard, Joan.
Tales from toddler hell : my life as a mom / Joan Leonard.
p. cm.
ISBN 0-88687-542-0 : $14.95
1. Motherhood—United States—Humor. 2. Mothers—United States—Humor. 3. Child rearing—United States—Humor.
I. Title.
HQ759.L46   1991
306.874'3—dc20   91-7601
CIP

Pharos Books
A Scripps Howard Company
200 Park Avenue
New York, N.Y. 10166

Printed in the United States of America

10 9 8 7 6 5 4 3 2 1

Pharos Books are available at special discounts on bulk purchases for sales promotions, premiums, fundraising or educational use. For details, contact the Special Sales Department, Pharos Books, 200 Park Avenue, New York, NY 10166.

For my family
May our spirit ever wave

▲.■.▲.■.▲.■.▲.■.▲.■.▲.■.▲.■.▲.■.▲.■.▲.■

Contents

▲.■.▲.■.▲

1. Why We Did It 11

2. Lamazed-Out 17

3. How We Survived Our First Night Out....... 23

4. Post-Baby Beach Days 31

5. Venice with a Stroller 35

6. Reflections on a Second Child 43

7. Aerobics for a Mom............................... 49

8. "It's Only a Two-Hour Flight!".................. 57

9. I Remember Slow Dancing....................... 63

10. The Girls We Used to Be......................... 69

11. Perfect Children I Have Known and Loathed...**75**

12. A Weekend Alone **81**

13. We Never Argued Until We Had Children....**87**

14. "Mommie and Me" **93**

15. Dining at Home with the Family...............**99**

16. Happy Endings **105**

Tales from Toddler Hell

Why We Did It

*M*y husband and I had a pretty nice life before we decided to have children. Nice house, nice cars, nice retirement savings plan. We'd spend our Saturday afternoons browsing through antique stores and our Sunday mornings in bed with the newspapers and each other. On a whim we'd run off to the movies, to a new restaurant, to the Algarve region of Portugal. We'd plan elaborate dinner parties with friends and discuss at great length the texture of the Fettucine Alfredo and the bouquet of the Chardonnay.

But we couldn't leave well enough alone, could we?

It's hard to remember exactly when it happened, but somewhere around the third year we were together, my husband and I started actually *noticing* children—as if for the first time.

We suddenly saw them on the streets of New York and on the tennis courts of Long Island. They cropped up at our favorite cafés, on the shores of Fire Island, at Kennedy Airport. Although there were always a few kids that were clearly obnoxious, most of them began to appear. . . well, cute. That was the first stage. In the past kids just seemed to be a minor irritation—a background noise in restaurants, screams on airplanes, whines at the supermarket. But then they had to turn cute on us. I started noticing their cute little snowsuits and their adorable baby sneakers. My husband actually talked to them while he waited on line at hardware stores on Saturday mornings.

Stage two came a few months later. We casually—and cautiously—brought up the *concept* of children in our daily conversation. When we went house-hunting, for example, we'd say that IF we ever decided to have children, that upstairs bedroom could sure work as a nice nursery. On our vacations to Europe we'd stare at the adorable Norwegian toddlers in matching ski sweaters sitting in our train compartment and mention how important it would be IF we ever had children to expose them to other cultures. And on a quiet Christmas morning that year when the snow lay flat like carpet and the frost closed around the windows of our new house, we sat under our tree—just the two of us with our expensive presents and our fresh-ground coffee in our porcelain mugs—and we WANTED children.

Then a few of our friends began to start a family. That was when we noticed the bizarre changes that seemed to come over new parents. In the past usually tasteful and gracious, they now came to our dinners obsessed with their newborns' bowel habits, which they described in excruciating detail over the main course. Also, my husband and I couldn't help but notice a marked downswing in their appearance; we're talking slovenly in some cases. A bit of spit-up here, a beard stubble there—and then there was their eyes: glazed and maniacal, I suppose, because of their lack of sleep for the past six months—or so they claimed. They were a bit snappish with each other, too, and had to get home by eleven.

Well, that was certainly not going to happen to us, my husband and I promised each other in those early days of wishful thinking. Stage three consisted of our careful but fruitless plans for having two perfect children in our perfect house while still excelling at our jobs and keeping our perfect marriage.

We did, of course, discuss some of the obstacles involved. We had been married long enough, for example, to know that the two of us were not cut from the same bolt of cloth. Dark and Mediterranean and passionate about everything, my husband came from generations of hot-blooded Italians who loved cooking and opera, while I hailed from staid Nordic Wisconsin farmers with a strong work ethic and a desire to polka at weddings.

When my husband gets angry, he yells and thrashes around for a while, then forgets all about it. When I get angry, I purse my lips, lower my eyes, and remain mute for three weeks. I am always on time; my husband is always late. I like English Country; he likes Roman Baroque. I am precise; he is vague. I am up-tight, he is earthy. Still, we remained optimistic about having children. Despite our differences, we both had the same general views on raising kids. Besides, we both thought we'd be able to preserve our present way of life even though we were going to have children.

Of course we were dead wrong. When our daughter Annie was born, we tried valiantly to keep our old life-style intact, but we knew within two days of bringing her home from the hospital that we were fighting a losing battle. Still, a few months later we bought tickets to the New York City Opera in a vain attempt to salvage our old life-style. But Annie was still nursing and that night my brand-new battery-operated breast pump broke in the ladies-room stall and *The Magic Flute* is a four-hour opera—and, well, it's not a pretty story.

When our son Alex was born eighteen months later, my husband and I knew we were goners. By the time he learned to walk, our house looked permanently like wartorn Libya and all four of us resembled Romanian refugees.

Our life has changed so radically that even we are dumfounded. Our elegant dinner parties have become Thursday-night family specials at the Ground Round, where children pay a penny per pound and a clown entertains the kids. My husband's beloved BMW has been traded in for a family sedan with kiddie locks and two space-age car seats separated by empty cardboard juice containers. Our oak buffet in the dining room has become the downstairs changing table, and we are on our second VCR—the first having been broken by a damp Zweiback lodged in back.

And we have both aged: oh, yes. They say children keep

you young—that may be—but they keep you *looking* old. We are, it seems, always tired. It has become a personal crusade for each of us to get seven hours of uninterrupted sleep. But usually we take turns getting up in the middle of the night—either because Alex is teething or Annie has a nightmare or it's thundering or the dog next door is barking.

Then there is the guilt. In the beginning we felt guilty putting our newborn in a wind-up swing for one hour because Good Parents would have rocked the baby and crooned lullabies in her ear instead of being so selfish as to want to eat dinner. I feel guilty dressing Alex in his sister's pink hand-me-down sleepers, and my husband feels guilty for not taking Annie to the petting zoo more often. We both feel guilty putting on *The Little Mermaid* and lining up their highchairs inches from the TV on Friday night so we can sit in the living room, drinking a glass of wine— because Good Parents would be dining with their children even on a Friday night.

We now have two children who we believe will be toddlers for the rest of their lives—although my neighbor claims, from experience, that they will only be toddlers for another twelve years, at which time they will instantly turn into teenagers—a condition that, she insists, is even worse. I doubt it. What could be worse than driving down the Bronx River Parkway past abandoned buildings and roving packs of drug addicts and having Annie and Alex both announce they have to go pottie. Now. ("Poopers, Mom!") What could be worse than having a sitter say "Well, Annie took this little pill but I called Poison Control and they said it's probably nothing." What could be worse than loading one kid into the car and finding out the other one has disappeared into the road and is running around the blind curve at that very minute?

And yet, there are times when things sort of jell—when everything comes together for a moment of glory: when the double stroller opens the way it's supposed to, or we discover triple diaper coupons at Kiddie City, or we find a sitter who actually *likes* the children and is even available on Saturday nights. Of course, there are Christmas mornings. Despite the broken ornaments and the torn wrapping paper and the spilled orange juice, Christmas mornings are nice.

And do we miss the old life—the afternoons browsing in antique shops and wandering through museums and planning dinner parties? The winter vacations in the Caribbean and the summer weekends in the wine country? Do we miss drinking with glass goblets and a clean car and eight hours of uninterrupted sleep each night?

Hardly ever.

Lamazed-Out

We are of course late to our first Lamaze class.
And, although we are both really looking forward to having a baby in our lives, neither of us is looking
forward to these six evening sessions on childbirth in
someone's living room—learning how to Deal with the
Pain. For the past seven months my husband and I have
been able to dream about becoming parents in rather
abstract terms. Tonight, however, we would be forced to
confront the reality of it all. I, for one, would much rather
prepare for the birth of my child by lingering, as I've been
doing lately, in the freshly painted nursery each morning
and rearranging cute little baby outfits on cute little hang-
ers in the closet. My husband, who has always been
skittish around hospitals and turns green at the mere
mention of medical procedures, is actually dreading to-

night's Lamaze class. Although he is in most ways a thoroughly modern man, now that I am pregnant I can tell he longs for the days when men were men and women had babies alone. He wants childbirth to be like the 1960s sitcom childbirths, when expectant fathers like Rob Petrie and Darrin Stephens paced in the waiting room while their wives made us laugh uproariously all the way to commercial break—after which adorable babies miraculously appeared in their mothers' arms.

We pull into the driveway of a low ranch, and Marge greets us at the door. She is a cheerful, efficient-looking nurse who has been teaching the Lamaze Method for fifteen years. Marge has had eight children and lived to tell about it.

"We were just getting started," she says brightly and hands us nametags with a yellow stork in the corner and "Hi" next to our names. I dutifully put mine on; my husband crumbles his up and shoves it into my purse when Marge turns her back.

We join the other five couples sitting in a circle in the living room; ceiling fans are on high. It is a hot, airless Monday night, and no one looks thrilled to be here except for one man who sits with a yellow legal pad on his lap while his wife fans herself with Marge's Lamaze pamphlet.

"Twins," he whispers as we take a seat next to him.

I glance around the room, checking out the women. We are all in our third trimester, and some of us look better than others. I decide I am toward the bottom of the scale, looking nowhere near as radiant as the honey blonde in a silk overblouse or the executive in the dress-for-success maternity suit who is just closing her briefcase. I do, however, look a little more put-together than the woman in bedroom slippers and a muumuu across the room.

It becomes obvious that my husband is not the only reluctant Lamaze coach here at Marge's house. In fact, many of the men sit glumly with arms folded in front of them, looking like they are ready to spring out of the room given the slightest chance.

Marge takes her seat by a gigantic poster showing the female reproductive organs in incredible four-color detail. My husband stares at it in horror.

"Childbirth," begins Marge dramatically, "does not have to mean pain and confusion. It can, in fact, be a beautiful, positive experience." She pauses and smiles beatifically. "Childbirth with dignity: That's what this class is all about." She inhales deeply, then purses her lips and slowly exhales.

"I've just taken a deep cleansing breath, and already I feel relaxed. You will, too. Any questions before we begin?"

One anxious young woman raises her hand.

"When do they do the episiotomy?" she asks in strident tones.

A murmur of panic wafts through the crowd, the women looking at one another, the men looking confused. Husbands do not know what an episiotomy is—unlike their wives, who have been reading everything they could get their hands on relating to childbirth.

Marge does not welcome the question.

"We'll talk about that at the next session," she says calmly. "Right now I'd like us to make our introductions. Tell us a little about yourselves."

We go around the room—my husband limiting his introduction to name, rank, and serial number—while another couple drones on for ten minutes, telling us all about the moment of conception, their genetic history, and how much they paid for their house.

Marge then gives us a course outline. In future sessions, she explains, we will learn relaxation exercises, breathing methods, and how to recognize the three stages of labor. The last session will be sort of a field trip for the condemned: a tour of the labor and delivery rooms at our local hospital. Our husbands, promises Marge, will learn to coach us into a relatively pain-free, drug-free childbirth.

"I'll believe *that* when I see it," mutters the woman in bedroom slippers. Her husband looks up from the crossword puzzle he's been working on.

Marge frowns. "It is time for a break," she says. "When we return we will see a video on childbirth. But now please help yourselves to some nutritious snacks in the kitchen." She raises her arms like a cheerleader. "And think positive!" she shouts.

We all rise from our folding chairs and wander over to the low-salt crackers and skim milk in paper cups. We make smalltalk for a moment, then get down to basics and exchange horror stories about childbirth.

"My sister-in-law," begins one woman, "was in labor for three days and then had to have a cesarean section."

"Oh yeah?" countered another. "Well, my neighbor's daughter had a whole face of broken blood vessels after she had her baby. Especially on her nose. Now she looks like W. C. Fields, and she doesn't even drink."

As if on cue, the men begin to drift away and end up huddled together in Marge's mud room, where they discuss how the Mets are doing this year.

Marge breaks things up and calls us back into the living room. While she dims the lights and turns on the VCR, she announces that this is an actual birth that was videotaped at her hospital last year. The credits roll, and we see a woman in a birthing room wallpapered with daisies. She is breathing serenely while her husband practices effleurage on her belly. She concentrates on her focal point: two ceramic bunnies placed on the dresser. The words STAGE ONE: EARLY LABOR flash across the screen. The class begins to relax a bit. This isn't, after all, so bad. Soon there is a fade-in to STAGE TWO: LABOR. She isn't so serene any more and seems somewhat irritated by her husband's effleurage. She takes several deep cleansing breaths, but it doesn't look like it's helping much. Finally she slaps her husband's hand away and pushes him off the bed. Cut to STAGE THREE: TRANSITION. The woman, now sweating, her hair damp, is on her hands and knees, blowing and panting furiously. There is a close-up of a fetal monitor recording her contractions, which seem to be doubling up rapidly. Her husband is shouting out directions to breathe.

At this point I feel my husband groping for my hand. We exchange glances, and even in the dark I can see that he is pale. I too am pale as well as scared. How will we manage this?, I think. And why did we decide to have children in the first place? The whole class is riveted to the screen, and I begin to doubt Marge's judgment for showing this kind of film to first-time expectant mothers and fathers—especially when it is obvious that no one in this class is exactly a profile in courage.

Now the woman is in the delivery room, and all of a sudden doctors and nurses are fluttering around and her husband is behind her, dressed in green scrubs. "Push!" he yells and then counts to ten, and the next moment a messy, bloody, gorgeous baby is pushed out and held up to the screen. The baby, eyes squeezed shut and fists clenched in rage, is howling and the new mother is laughing and the new father is crying and the nurses are cheering. "What a great day!" the doctor whispers, placing the infant in the mother's arms. She kisses the baby on the forehead and her husband rips off his mask and buries his head in his wife's neck. Fade out.

Marge turns on the lights. There's not a dry eye in the house, and for a moment we all forget about episiotomies and cesareans and fetal monitors. We are remembering only the baby that has just come tumbling out into life— and now I realize why Marge, in her wisdom, decided to show us the movie. All of us, I am sure, are just as apprehensive as we were before, but now we have been reminded that there is a purpose, a reason, a reward much greater than the process itself. Despite our fears, we know that the future will be worth the present.

My husband and I say goodnight to Marge, feeling strangely exhilarated, and on impulse decide to go out for pizza to commemorate the occasion.

Suddenly we have a lot to celebrate.

How We Survived
Our First Night
Out

▲•■•▲•■•

7:15 P.M. Waiting for the babysitter. My husband and I sit perched on the sofa, holding five-month-old Annie. This will be the first time since her birth that we will be leaving her in the hands of an official babysitter. Until now my parents have been only too happy to look after her from time to time. Tonight, however, they are out of town and it is our wedding anniversary. So, determined to celebrate in style, we have made a dinner reservation at an expensive French restaurant and we have booked Jennifer, a highly recommended, reserved-a-month-in-advance, sixteen-year-old babysitter.

We have been preparing for her arrival all day. Remembering my own babysitting days—when I was a snoopy high school student—I have made a clean sweep of the house, hiding questionable magazines, questionable videos, credit card statements, liquor bottles, prescription pills, and contraceptive paraphernalia. Meanwhile, my husband has spent the afternoon working on the emergency-phone-number list. On the refrigerator, held with magnets, is a large sheet of paper with the following emergency numbers written in red Magic Marker:

Poison Control
Police
Rescue
Fire Department
Pediatrician
Pediatrician's back-up
Next-door neighbor
Insurance representative

And a few spaces down, in bold capital letters:

WHERE WE'LL BE:

"I think Pediatrician should come first," I had said after reading over the list. "After all, in an emergency you'd want a doctor."

"No, no, no," my husband said. "Poison Control." I knew he had a thing about poison. He has already called Poison Control several times since Annie was born. There was the time she held an ant trap to her mouth ("Not poisonous, sir, just some peanut butter in there") and the time she tasted some diaper-rash ointment ("Not enough to do any harm"). The last time he had accidentally given her a double dose of children's cough syrup. They recognize his voice now. We finally compromised by making Poison Control number one and Pediatrician number two.

▲   ▲   ▲

7:30 P.M. The sitter arrives. My husband and I rush to the door and in walks gum-chewing Jennifer carrying a knapsack and a can of diet soda.

"Hi," she says, brushing past us and setting down her things. "So this is Annie!" She takes Annie from me and puts her on her lap. Knowing full well Annie hates being picked up by strangers, I say, "She's been kind of fussy today." My voice dwindles off as I see Annie looking up at Jennifer with adoration. I feel a twinge. Has my daughter forgotten me already?

"Noooo, Annie's a good baby," Jennifer says in triumph, kissing her on the cheek. Germs, I think absently.

My husband stirs. "Jennifer," he says in his most authoritative voice, "I have a list to show you. In the kitchen." My husband follows her, pausing in front of me. "Too young," he says through gritted teeth.

"Well, here it is." He stands next to the refrigerator like a high school history teacher pointing to a map, and reads aloud the phone numbers as Jennifer slowly chews her gum and eyes the bowl of potato chips on the counter next to the ipecac syrup.

"Any questions?"

"Just one," Jennifer answers. "Do you have a VCR?"

7:45 P.M. En route to restaurant. "I don't like it. I just don't like it," my husband mutters as we drive. "I can't believe we are trusting our most prized possession to that, that, that—TEENAGER!"

"She'll be fine," I say with a conviction I don't feel. "Everyone uses her and thinks she's great."

"She wasn't paying attention to my list," argued my husband. "And when I took her down in the basement she didn't even look at the fuse box."

"That might have been overdoing it a bit," I said gently.

"Overdoing it? What if there's an electrical storm tonight?"

8:00 P.M. Expensive French Restaurant. We are seated at a tiny candlelit table for two. The waiter brings us champagne. We are going to have fun if it kills us. My husband raises a glass for a toast. "Happy Anniversary, Darling," he says. We clink glasses. "Think we should call the sitter?" We decide to wait until we order. The waiter again approaches the table and begins to describe in minute detail the canard à l'orange. But wait! That's the phone ringing! My husband holds up his hand to silence the waiter. From across the room we watch with frozen anticipation as the maître d' answers at his station. The phone will be for us, we both know with dead certainty. It will be the sitter. I picture Annie hurtling down the basement stairs, landing with a dull thud on the concrete floor, while my husband pictures her drinking toilet-bowl cleaner in the bathroom. We both half stand at the table, poised to race to the phone. The maître d' smiles into the phone and jots down something on paper and hangs up. We sit down again and the waiter continues his litany of French delicacies.

▲   ▲   ▲

8:30 P.M. We decide it's time to call the sitter. I stand at the pay phone, clutching the receiver—my only link to our daughter. Play it cool, I tell myself.

"Hi, Jennifer. Just calling to, ah, check in." I laugh apologetically.

"Uh huh."

"So. How's Annie doing?"

"Fine."

"Fine? Good!" I say too heartily. "Ah, how did she eat?"

"Fine."

"Fine? Good! Did she fuss at all?"

"No, she was fine."

"Fine? Good! Look Jennifer, could you expand on that a little?"

"Huh?"

"Just kidding, ha, ha." Calm down, I tell myself. "Ah, did she go to sleep all right? My husband says I'm the only one who can get her to sleep..."

"She's asleep. She's fine."

"Great!" I say cheerfully.

I return to our table and repeat the conversation to my husband.

"Something's wrong. Let's go home," my husband says. We choke down our canard à l'orange, guzzle the last drops of champagne, and pay the check.

9:30 P.M. We walk in the door and race into the den, where Jennifer is reading *Romeo and Juliet* Cliff Notes and watching *Dirty Dancing* at the same time.

She looks up, puzzled. "That was a quick dinner," she says.

My husband lunges at her. I pull him back by his arm. "Everything all right?" I ask brightly.

"Fine." She says, pulling out her video from the VCR and shrugging on her jacket.

10:00 P.M. My husband and I sit in the den, having put away Jennifer's cola can and the bowl of chips. Suddenly I spot a tiny white pill lying on the floor next to Annie's infant seat. I point to it in horror.

"Oh my God!" screams my husband from his recliner.

I pick it up, a thousand thoughts racing through our heads. She has drugged Annie, I think. I read about a day care center that did that, my husband says. Our babysitter is a drug addict, I moan. Then I look closer at the pill, smell it, and finally lick it. I look up at my husband in chagrin.

"A Tic-tac," I say. "Peppermint, I think."

11:00 P.M. In our bedroom. We have checked in on Annie, who is sleeping peacefully. She is wearing the right sleeper. She is in clean diapers. She has drunk her bottle of milk. We chuckle together, in the safety of our bed, over our evening out—how we overreacted, how we mistrusted Jennifer, how next time we would be much more relaxed, and perhaps even make it to dessert and coffee. And yet, although I don't mention it to my husband, there is a tiny part of me that still resents Jennifer's efficiency. Annie had gone to sleep with a stranger just as easily as she had slept for me, her mother. I realize I'm not as indispensable as I had thought—or hoped. I turn off the light with a sigh.

▲ ▲ ▲

3:00 A.M. I awake to hear Annie's cry. I jump out of bed and hurry to her room. Although some babies are constantly up at night, we had been blessed with a baby who slept through the night ever since she was two months old. This was the first time since then that Annie had awakened at three in the morning.

As I peek into her crib, Annie opens her eyes without squinting and stares at me solemnly. I lean over and stroke her forehead for a minute, wondering if I should pick her up or not. Suddenly she gives me a huge smile, puts her thumb in her mouth, and closes her eyes. I tiptoe back to our bedroom.

"She okay?" mumbles my husband groggily.

"She's just fine," I say. "She just wanted to make sure I was back."

"Huh?" my husband said.

"Never mind," I say smugly, and turn off the light.

Post-Baby
Beach Days

*M*y husband and I have finally crossed the threshold into middle age. It comes to me in a flash today at the beach as we stagger across the sand searching for a good spot—my husband looking like a dazed nomad carrying umbrella, cooler, towels, port-o-crib, and sand chairs and I clutching nine-month-old Annie in one arm and a bag of potato chips and diaper bag in the other. It is a far cry from our early dating days, when the two of us used to come to the beach bringing nothing more than a towel and our passion.

"Here!" I shout back to my husband, who has just dropped the umbrella twenty feet behind me. The spot we choose is one we would have avoided years ago: directly in front of the lifeguard and only a few feet from the water's edge so we could watch the baby. Like us, most of the crowd gathered here are families with young children and enough beach paraphernalia to last weeks. On their perimeter are older couples and singles without children, sitting on blankets reading magazines and listening to radios. And far off in the distance, near deserted sand dunes, young couples lie flush with the horizon, gazing at each other passionately.

I remember those sand dunes. My husband and I, when we first met, used to spend hours at this same beach by those same dunes. The romance of the hot sultry beach weighed heavy in our imagination in those days. We'd take long walks—I in my bikini and he in his surfer shorts—occasionally taking a dip in the waves. Sometimes he would stop in midsentence and—for no reason at all—kiss me ardently, then continue talking. And while time may have sweetened the details, I can, even now, remember an afternoon à la Burt Lancaster and Deborah Kerr in *From Here to Eternity* when we emerged from the water, laughing—I collapsed on the sand and he dropped to his knees suddenly, then enfolded me in his arms while the surf pounded suggestively in the background.

I think of that scene while my husband and I argue over who gets the deluxe sand chair and who gets the cheap one (He wins; his back hurt from carrying everything). We begin to arrange our equipment: we open the umbrella, assemble the port-o-crib, put the baby in the port-o-crib, put the port-o-crib under the umbrella, get out the sun block, put on our sun visors, and plop down in the sand chairs in exhaustion. There we sit—I in my conservative tank suit to hide the stretch marks and he in his large swim trunks—watching the parade of nubile young men and women walk by us, their fannies hovering directly at our eye level.

"I'm starving," he says. "Is it too early for lunch?"

I look at my watch: 10:45 A.M. He hands me a sandwich and we sit silently chewing while we watch the show in front of us. We used to go to the beach to escape reality, to get a tan, to swim, to make out. Now we go to eat.

What has happened to our romantic trips to the shore?, I think as I pass him the bag of potato chips. And why is it the older you get the more you bring to the beach? There seems to be a connection there, something to do with sand chairs and the loss of passion.

Maybe I'm being too sensitive, but to me, going to the beach used to symbolize all of the romance and passion and freedom the two of us shared from the beginning. It was a place to whisper dreams, to walk and talk for hours without interruptions. Even after that first blush of love, my husband and I would come to the beach summer after summer—each year bringing larger blankets and more supplies—and there we would discuss our plans for travel, for marriage, for a home.

Today, ten years later, I still love to go to the beach with him. Unfortunately these days long lazy walks are the last thing on our minds. Much to our surprise, we have somehow turned into official adults with responsibilities like mortgage payments and cesspool upkeep and attic insulation, and our talk reflects those mundane subjects. We are beginning to worry about high cholesterol and receding hairlines and cellulite. And now that we have finally become first-time parents, we have added topics like diaper absorbency and bowel-movement consistency to our beach conversation. While we both admit that our days don't really begin until we get a smile from our daughter, we also face the grim reality that our priorities have been altered forever. Lately, for example, being close to the restrooms seems more important than privacy behind the dunes.

I sigh as I watch my husband dozing in the sun. His face is beginning to look peculiarly streaked from the sun block he had applied unevenly. It is definitely time to leave. Annie is getting cranky, the canvas on my sand chair has snapped, and the cooler is leaking.

Still, passion moves in strange ways. I have nudged my husband awake and the two of us have just walked Annie down to the water's edge to rinse her off when my husband suggests a walk on the beach.

"I'm too tired," I whine.

"Come on," he coaxes. "I'll carry Annie."

And so we walk, while not hand in hand, at least heart in heart. Once the surf causes a mist to cover us and once Annie shrieks with glee as she watches me return a Frisbee to two teenagers. And just before we turn around to head back to our sand chairs, my husband suddenly shifts Annie to his other hip, grabs my shoulder with his free hand and—for no reason at all—kisses me full on the lips.

"Life's not so bad, is it?" he whispers.

I look into his eyes, then into my daughter's, then at the horizon where the sun lay low against the dunes.

Not bad at all.

Venice with a Stroller

▲ ● ■ ● ▲ ● ■ ●

*M*y husband and I remember every detail of our first trip to Venice. We had been traveling throughout Europe for weeks, but from the moment we emerged from the St. Lucia train station and were nearly blinded by the reflection of the water on the Grand Canal, we knew that Venice was going to be different from anything we'd seen so far. For days we wandered through the narrow streets, drinking espresso at Florian's in St. Mark's Square, eating in tiny trattorias, and watching the gondoliers drift by crumbling buildings layered with alfresco paintings. Almost drunk from the richness of it all, we vowed to return some day to its magic.

Five years later, after we became parents, we decided to go back to Europe—this time with ten-month-old Annie. Our friends with children tried to warn us against traveling with a baby. After all, they argued, one had to make certain adjustments with children. Europe was one of those adjustments. It was time to think about a more traditional family vacation instead. They didn't have to tell us; we had sat in their darkened living room watching their vacation slides evolve, in past few years, from wide-angle shots of charming chateaus in Bordeaux and rolling hills in Tuscany to close-ups of the Petting Zoo and Yogi Bear Family Campgrounds. As the carousel click-clicked through endless shots of kiddie pools, life-sized puppets, and adorable fawns being bottle-fed, my husband and I smirked at each other in disdain. Not for us a change in life-style. Not for us a sellout to parenthood. Not for us Sesame Place in Pennsylvania. We would travel to Europe with our baby. What's more, we would take Annie to our favorite city in the world. We would return in triumph to Venice.

And so it is with utmost confidence and high spirits that the three of us emerge from the train station into the brilliant sunshine of Venice. And once again we gasp at its splendor as it lies below us. This time, however, instead of knapsacks on our back and Birkenstock sandals on our feet, we carry Annie, a port-o-crib, stroller, one large suitcase, diaper bag, and camera bag. On our feet are sturdy walking shoes and breathable cotton socks. Undaunted, we unfold the stroller, strap Annie in with her seat belt, adjust our luggage, and prepare to greet our beloved city.

This is when we notice the steps. We now discover that there are twenty-seven steps from the St. Lucia station to the entrance of the *motoscafo*. Five years ago my husband

and I had skipped down those steps, laughing gaily and
holding hands. Now we stand, riveted in place, staring at
the stroller and then lifting our eyes to the distance and
taking in endless picturesque bridges which make up our
favorite city in the world. A statistic comes to mind from
some travel book I had been reading: 400. There are 400
bridges in Venice. I stop my mind from trying to compute
how many steps that equals.

Like a scene from a bad silent movie, we jump into action:
Unbuckle Annie's seat belt. Lift Annie out of stroller. Fold
stroller. Husband carries stroller down steps. Wife carries
Annie down steps. Husband returns up steps to retrieve
luggage, port-o-crib, etc. By the time we reach the *motoscafo*
entrance, it feels as if we had been in Venice a month.

We decide to ask the man in the booth what the policy is
regarding bringing strollers aboard the boat. As usual, the
Italian policy is no policy.

"If it's not crowded, it's all right," the man says to my
husband in Italian. "But if it's crowded..." His voice
dwindles off and he shrugs his shoulders sadly.

We decide to take our chances and push our way aboard.
We needn't have worried. Although it is crowded, a third
of the passengers jump up to offer me a seat, while my
husband stands, clutching a pole, his legs wrapped around
the port-o-crib.

After the boat rams itself into the pier at San Zaccaria, the
crowd opens a path for the stroller like the parting of the
Red Sea. I push Annie out while my husband manages to
fight his way through the mob at the back of the boat and
disembark a moment later.

I consult my map and see that it is a short walk—three bridges—to our hotel. My husband learns to amend the stroller/bridge process by simply lifting the stroller with Annie in it and, with a Neanderthal grunt, stagger up and over each bridge while Annie thumps his head with her bottle. By the end of the week he will have black-and-blue marks down the outside of his right leg from his hip to his ankle.

It is another struggle trying to get us all in the tiny, four-by-four-square hotel elevator without having to lift Annie out of the stroller. We end up pushing Annie into the elevator, then partially collapsing the stroller while our baby folds into a semifetal position. My husband and I then edge ourselves inside on tiptoes, lunging over the stroller and bracing our hands on the opposite wall. The luggage and port-o-crib go on Annie's lap.

Once inside our room, we fling everything on the floor, let Annie out of the stroller, and flop on the bed in exhaustion. Annie crawls into the bathroom, where she discovers the bidet.

Battered but not defeated, we decide to try dinner. My husband, raised in Italy, has been looking forward to returning to certain Venetian restaurants he has thoroughly researched and painstakingly listed in his notebook.

After a long walk (six bridges), we enter the Gardinetto, where the owner greets us and pretends to remember us from five years ago. My husband is relieved to find that the restaurant still makes homemade gnocci—"lighter than air"—on Thursdays, and today is Thursday. He and the owner begin an enthusiastic discussion of the dinner menu while our daughter begins her familiar low-pitched whine indicating restlessness. Offering bread sticks does not help. Juice does not help. Pellegrino designer water direct from the bottle does not help. I pick her up and hold her on my lap until she manages to slither down my leg and land on the exquisite marble floor. By the time my husband finishes ordering, Annie is heading toward the canal. As the rest of the diners watch her crawl past them, it becomes painfully clear to all of us that it is time to change her diaper. Did I mention that Italian diapers don't seem to have that good ol' American absorbency? This is an inconvenience when we're talking number one and a disaster when we're talking number two. We're talking number two here.

Of course, even a fresh Italian diaper would be appreciated at this moment—but, alas, we have forgotten to bring diapers to the Gardinetto. My husband meanwhile grabs Annie by the armpits just as she is about to take a dip and makes a beeline to the men's room, almost colliding with the waiter, who is bringing homemade gnocci, lighter than air, to our table. My husband closes his eyes briefly as the waiter passes him, then enters the men's room. A moment later he returns to our table, holding Annie in her new makeshift diaper. She wears two plastic bags knotted on each side and stuffed with wads of Italian toilet paper. I restrain her in the stroller once again, and my husband sits down to eat.

But somehow the mood is gone. We pay our bill, walk to a pharmacy where we purchase diapers, stop at Wendy's for a burger and a kiddie meal, and turn in early (eight bridges total).

After that, our days fall into a routine. No more elegant restaurants at dusk. In the morning we plot our route by way of the fewest bridges. As we walk, we watch Annie out of the corner of an eye to see when her eyelids grow heavy. As soon as she nods off, we immediately drop to the nearest café chair, like participants in Musical Chairs.

"Due Cappucini," my husband whispers to the passing waiter. While Annie naps, we can settle back with our coffee and relax. We look across the table at one another, and for a few moments we are back in the Venice we remember. All too soon, though, Annie stirs, gripping the sides of her stroller and rocking back and forth, a gentle hint that it is time to roll.

Annie is at her worst on our last night in Venice. She has not slept during our siesta that afternoon, choosing instead to kick rhythmically at the sides of her port-o-crib while we attempted to nap. It is now 9:00 P.M. and we are still pushing the stroller and Annie is still awake.

As we walk down the Riva degli Schiavoni, my husband points out the Danieli, the grandest hotel in Venice as well as a stunning landmark. Five years ago my husband and I had walked reverently through the lobby, and now suddenly I want to see it again. I ask my husband to walk back and forth with Annie while I use the restroom.

I enter the hotel and a blast of cool air greets me. To my left is a huge lobby with Oriental rugs and brocade sofas. To my right is the writing room—filled with Queen Anne desks with individual lamps. Ahead of me is a sweeping staircase, and at the top, around the corner, is the Ladies' room. Inside the walls, ceiling, and floors are pink marble.

There is a stack of neat, ironed linen napkins next to each sink. No paper towels for the Danieli. The wastebasket, I notice, is also pink marble. I stare at my disheveled reflection in the gilt-framed mirror while two elegant women in silk Ungaro dresses and high heels drift in, chatting in rapid Italian. They take out lipstick from tiny metallic evening bags while I use a linen towel to wipe formula off my shirt. I quickly leave. I am really feeling sorry for myself now, but just for good measure I linger outside the hotel's restaurant on the balcony, where well-dressed couples sit at candlelit tables looking out onto the Grand Canal.

As I descend the stairs, however, I hear the familiar sounds of my daughter, giggling and shrieking beneath me. There on the Oriental rugs of the Hotel Danieli is Annie, with my husband and two bellhops crouched around her, all three of them laughing with her. The stroller has left marks on the marble floor. In any other country we would have been asked to leave, but this was Italy, where children reign supreme. And now an elderly couple, who have been reading newspapers and sipping coffee, come over to enjoy our daughter. Annie finally stands up, lets go of the cocktail table, and totters toward me. The bellhop reaches for her as she falls.

"*Buona fortuna,* eh?" he says as he brushes the hair from her eyes.

My husband and I exchange glances and nod our heads. For a moment I forget about the spit-up on my shoulder and the skid marks from the stroller. Venice, I admit, is not a city for strollers, and I'm sure that our future vacations, like our friends' trips before us, will be more child-oriented than this one. But as we look down on our daughter, who is being spoon-fed the steamed milk from the elderly woman's cappucino, my husband and I will swear that Venice is still a place of magic—for all three of us.

We leave the Danieli, our spirits lift. The ornate street lamps come on, and we can see the silhouettes of the lions of St. Mark's and the island of Murano past the Grand Canal. Somewhere we hear the strains of "O Sole Mio" being sung by an ambitious gondolier for the tourists in his gondola. I glance down at my map. Only four bridges left to get back to our hotel.

Buona fortuna.

Reflections on a Second Child

▲▪▲▪▲▪

It is five in the morning when I hear a gurney being wheeled toward my room. I'm awake anyway, unable to sleep and waiting for my three-day-old son to be brought in for his feeding. When his sister was born, I had been lucky enough to have the whole room to myself. This time it looks as if I will be getting a roommate. I am in no mood to chat—my breasts ache, my stitches hurt, and the excitement and anticipation I had felt with my first child seem to have dissipated more quickly with the arrival of my second. Well into parenthood, I find that my mind is on more mundane matters. My husband, for example, has been home with Annie for the past three days, and I can picture the house: laundry piled up, the sink stacked with dishes, no sheets to fit the borrowed bassinet. I worry that Annie is eating too many sweets, that her clothes are on

43

backward, that she is staying up past her bedtime. The next few months, I know from experience, will be filled with sleepless nights and zombielike days. At this moment the future seems too overwhelming to contemplate. I quickly draw the curtain around my bed and pretend to be asleep. I should have gone home yesterday, I think, as the gurney enters my room. But my doctor has advised me to spend another day in the hospital. "With a toddler at home, you need all the rest you can get," she declared with a smile.

I hear a nurse fluttering around the room while the new mother and father giggle in that almost drunken manner I recognize as the we-did-it-we-really-did-it euphoria experienced right after childbirth.

"Nothing is like the magic of the birth of your first child," the nurse says as she shuts the door behind her. Eighteen months ago she had said the same thing to me.

I hear a paper bag rustle and then the soft pop of a cork.

"Shh!" whispers the mother. "You'll wake up my roommate."

"So what?" booms her husband. "The whole world should wake up. Think she wants some champagne?"

"No. She must be asleep."

For a moment I consider shoving my water cup through the curtain.

There is a clink of glasses, more whispering, and as I lie here in the dark I find myself making the inevitable comparisons between the birth of my first child and the birth of my second.

I remember every detail of the first. My husband and I

had also celebrated with champagne. When they'd brought our daughter back to my room, we spent hours admiring her perfect nose and strong chin. We too had been giddy. After we'd talked long into the morning my husband had fallen asleep in the chair beside my bed.

This time, however, everything went faster. My water broke at midnight, and immediately following was a Lucy-and-Ricky-Ricardo-go-to-the-hospital scene. I made it to the delivery room just in time; before I knew it, Alex was born and we were cheering along with the nurses. While Annie's birth had taken on the tone of a religious experience, Alex's seemed more like a rowdy celebration of life. After my husband got me settled in my room I sent him home to relieve our neighbor (who had come to babysit) before Annie woke up to find both of us gone. The champagne was replaced with orange juice in a paper cup, brought in by the nurse.

"You're an old hand at this now, right?" she remarked.

I begin to doze on and off as the new mother and father's conversation comes through the curtain in waves:

HE: You were so great.

SHE: No, *you* were so great.

HE: He looks like you.

SHE: No, he looks like you.

HE: Here, Sweetheart, have some more champagne.

SHE: Thanks. You were so great.

HE: No, *you* were so great.

SHE: He looks like you.

HE: No, he looks like you.

The conversation sounds strangely familiar. No doubt my husband and I had said the same words after Annie was born. With Alex's birth, however, the conversation went more like this:

ME: We can put him in the hall for the time being.
MY HUSBAND: We'll need another car seat.
ME: We can use the dining-room buffet as his changing table.
MY HUSBAND: He looks like Winston Churchill.

Meanwhile I think of my return home in the morning, and I plan my list of things to mention to my husband when he calls: diapers size large, diapers size small, a bassinet sheet, a baby outfit, a large bag for all the free samples I've been sure to collect here. Last time I'd been too dewy-eyed to take advantage of the free diapers, milk bottles, formula, sterile water, diaper-rash ointment. Now an experienced mother, I started squirreling away the supplies from the beginning.

Finally my roommate's husband leaves and she picks up the phone.

"Hello, Cindy? I did it! Two hours ago! I feel great! A boy, seven pounds three ounces." She laughs into the phone. "You were right. I have already forgotten the labor."

After five more phone calls—all with the same basic script—the room is quiet again.

Suddenly my telephone rings. It is my husband.

"Is everything okay?" I ask anxiously.

"I couldn't sleep," he replies cheerfully. "I vacuumed and put the new car seat in the car."

I picture two car seats in the back seat of our tiny two-door hatchback.

"I can't find a sheet for the bassinet, and Annie picked some dandelions for you. She is wearing me out." He pauses. "I miss you."

"I miss you, too," I say softly.

"I've got some champagne chilling in the refrigerator—we'll celebrate tomorrow."

"We'll have to wait until the kids are asleep."

"'The kids,'" repeats my husband. "That's the first time we said that. Sounds good, doesn't it?"

"Sounds scary."

"Naw, you're just tired," he says. "Just think of all the stuff we can do together. We can play bridge. We can play touch football, and when we go on vacation we can take advantage of all those two-children-stay-free-with-parents hotel specials!"

We hang up and I lie back in bed, thinking about the fact that there are four of us now. My husband and I are no longer just a married couple with a child. Now we have two children who, for a while, will share the same toys and attend the same school and look across the dinner table at each other. Scenes from my childhood television sit-coms, like *Leave It to Beaver* and *Make Room for Daddy* flash through my mind. Will Annie and Alex shop together for my birthday card? Will they fight over who gets to borrow the car on Saturday night? Will they dance at each other's wedding? Is it possible they will remain as close as my sister and I have for almost thirty years?

I think of my roommate and decide that if the first child brings a kind of magic to his parents, then surely the second brings with him the bond of family—a sense of strength and continuity.

I hear the already familiar wail of my son as the nurse brings him into my room.

"He certainly is hungry," she says as she draws open the curtain. Alex's eyes are squeezed shut, his cheeks fat and smooth, his mouth open wide and trusting.

I think of the coming months of night feedings and the arguments over whose turn it will be to get up. I think of the small and large diapers in my shopping cart. I think of Alex teething at the same time Annie potty-trains. And I remember the nurse's comment as she handed me my son for the first time on an early gray morning three days ago.

"Twice blessed," she whispered.

Twice blessed, indeed.

Aerobics
for a Mom

▲ ▪ ▲ ▪

I am poised at the entrance of our local health club, clutching my brand-new gym bag, which holds my still-in-the-plastic-bag aerobic leotard, Y-back sports bra, high-top aerobic shoes, and breathable cotton socks. My two children sit in their double stroller, straining to get a peek inside the steamed-up glass doors out of which come well-toned men and women with serious haircuts.

I am about to take my first aerobics class and am more than a bit apprehensive, since the exercise revolution seems to have passed me by during the years I was having children. And although I truly believe that I get more exercise on any given morning at the nearby toddler park than any aerobics class I could imagine, that fact is, I *had* put on a few pounds after my daughter was born. To make matters worse, what remaining muscle tone I might have still had disappeared with the recent birth of my son.

Caring for two children only eighteen months apart had sort of kept me in a vacuum, and a scary pattern was beginning to develop to my daily life: Feed the kids lunch, feed myself lunch. Put the kids down for a nap, put myself down for a nap. Feed the kids a snack, feed myself a snack. I was beginning to look forward to midafternoon milk and cookies, not to mention cleaning my plate at dinnertime so I could have a Popsicle™ for dessert.

You might say I was ripe for the brochure that came in the mail offering a free introductory one-week health club membership. The brochure opened up to show long-limbed, narrow-hipped women reclining by the whirlpool, pumping iron, and jumping enthusiastically in an aerobics class; everyone looked like they were having so much *FUN*. But it was the photo of the large, sunny nursery that finally did it for me. The thought of being able to deposit my two toddlers in the hands of loving caretakers while I burned off fat next door was too much to resist. I made an appointment for the next day's aerobics class.

My husband tried to conceal his relief at my decision, although I could tell he thought it was a good idea. He had, on more than one occasion, come home early from work to find me watching *That Girl* reruns while finishing off a box of Trix. Perhaps I did need some diversion, he said. My husband, of course, had not put on a few pounds after the birth of our two children. His weight, in fact, had not varied since age eighteen, despite a quart of ice cream on Friday nights and pancakes with syrup on Sunday mornings. No, he would say, patting his still relatively flat stomach, as long as he played a little soccer once a week, he stayed pretty fit. Life is not fair, I would think, turning the channel to *Mission Impossible*.

A man in a three-piece suit carrying his gym bag, his hair still damp from a shower, holds the door for the stroller, and we enter the health club. Both kids' heads swivel from side to side as they try to take in what looks to me like the set of a bad sci-fi movie: arcane machines attached to computers line one wall, filled with grunting, sweating bodies contorted into bizarre shapes, some with legs weighted down with steel cables. Above them hang huge neon signs proclaiming, with exclamation marks, various areas: ABDOMINAL ROOM!, CARDIOLOGIST!, EUCA-LYPTUS SAUNA!, and around the corner NURSERY! right next door to AEROBICS ROOM!

It is in the nursery that I deposit my children; they immediately begin to dismantle a bookshelf of toys. After a litany of their likes and dislikes, including preferences on diapering ("Ma'am, we don't do diapers"), I am off to the locker room (WOMENS LOCKER ROOM!), where a doctor's-office-type scale greets me. I decide to forgo the scale. I get my locker opened and begin tearing open the plastic bags filled with my new aerobic garb. The leotard is harder to put on than maternity pantyhose ever were, and the sports bra cuts off most of my lung capacity, making it all but impossible to bend over to tie my new aerobic shoes. I manage to get it all on, though, and turn to face the mirror. I decide the sweat band would be overkill.

I am exhausted already. However, I take a deep breath and go off to find the AEROBICS ROOM! Already there are fifteen women of various ages, many of them dressed in neon leotards with lightning bolts running down their thighs. They sit, doing stretches or examining cuticles, waiting for our teacher. I take a spot in the back and try not to look at my reflection in the mirrors, which are everywhere.

Suddenly an incredibly lithe young woman with long blond hair breezes in, carrying an array of cassette tapes. She heads for the stereo system on the floor of her platform, bending from the waist. For the next few moments we watch her trim and muscular behind as she arranges the music. I am becoming very depressed. Then she turns, smiles, and says "Hi, ya, everyone. My name is Tiffany, and I'm your instructor for your Low-Impact-Jazz-Dance-Aerobics class." She pauses dramatically. "This is a beginner's class; any advanced students please take a spot in the back." There is a reshuffling and before I can move to the front, the music begins to pound from eight speakers. Hopes of being able to hear my children's cries next door are immediately dashed. I am flanked by a gum-chewing teen who is resting in the Chinese Splits and a woman twice my age who is putting on wrist and ankle weights.

Tiffany whirls around, jumps onto the raised platform, and crouches like a caged animal. Her smile fades. Her face begins to twist into a grotesque mask.

Leaping over the stereo system, she screams in midair "Five! Six! Seven! Eight!" and suddenly everyone is moving, miraculously following Tiffany's gestures in the mirror.

I am lost. Tiffany is shouting out directions like "Walk it high!" and "Swing it to the right!" while I am walking it low and swinging it to the left. Tiffany gallops off the platform, through the crowd. She jumps in front of me, her faces inches from mine. She stares at me balefully.

"Attitude!" she shouts, and leaps away to another victim.

And I thought we could be friends.

"Work those abs." She pounds her stomach, which is, I might add, already concave.

Tiffany changes the cassette to heavy reggae and demonstrates the next set.

"Okay, we're gonna step to the side, step to the side, grapevine, lunge, and then shimmy, shimmy, shimmy. Got it?" She tosses back her hair.

Shimmy? Did she say shimmy? Like we used to shimmy to Sam-the-Sham in sixth grade? Doesn't Tiffany know that I am a nursing mother? that my never substantial breasts at this very moment grow large with milk? I shimmy, shimmy, shimmy with great care.

Finally the music stops. I stand, sweat streaming down my eyes, holding my sides and gasping for breath. I did it, I actually made it through my first aerobics class. Guess those mornings at the toddler park got me in shape after all, I think smugly. Unfortunately, I am wrong. Tiffany peels off her cropped T-shirt, exposing her Diana Ross arms.

"All warmed up?" she says. "Then, Let's Work Out!" Leaping off the platform, she adds "Yeah!" for emphasis, and turns up the volume. The eight speakers tremble with music so loud and pulsating that it reminds me of rock

concerts I used to attend in the good old days before I had
children and cared about preserving my eardrums.

Tiffany jogs and jumps and lunges and kicks for the next
forty-five minutes until even the most advanced pupil
starts to fade. She makes us work those thighs and work
those pecs and work that butt. I begin to take perverse
pleasure out of watching my fellow exercisers slowly lose
enthusiasm, one by one, like contestants in a dance mara-
thon. I am happy to report that the gum-chewing teen
next to me has stopped several times, ostensibly to adjust
her sweat band or to tie her shoe, but I knew it was just a
cover so she could rest a minute here and a minute there.
By now she has even stopped chewing her gum.

Eventually it becomes clear that the only one in class left
who is still having a Real Good Time is Tiffany. In fact, the
ecstacy of it all, apparently, becomes too much for her, and
from time to time she must let it out. She shakes her head
like John Lennon and Paul McCartney did in "Twist and
Shout" and screams, "Whoo-oo-oo-oo!" At first I think it
is another routine. Work that head. Then of course I see
that Tiffany is just experiencing that HIGH one gets from
reaching her aerobic potential.

I, on the other hand, am experiencing that NUMBNESS
one gets from reaching her pain threshold. My breathing
has become wheezing and I am reduced to walking in place
and swinging my arms pathetically to the left and right.

Finally it is over. I glance in the mirror. My face is
covered with blotches of bright red, my glasses have slid
down my nose, and my underpants are peeking out from
my leotard. My sports bra, however, is still riveted in

place. The music mercifully stops and Tiffany says "Great Workout!" and collects her cassette tapes.

Just as I am about to drag myself out of the exercise room—on my hands and knees, if necessary—someone taps me on the shoulder. It is Tiffany, and she is smiling kindly at me. Evidently the evil spirit of aerobics no longer possesses her body and she is back to her old self.

"Not bad for the first time," she says.

I look at her in disbelief.

"Really. I was in worse shape than you when I started aerobics. After my three kids were born (Kids? How can she look like that with three *kids*?) I used to sit around the house watching TV and eating junk food, believe it or not."

Hard to believe.

"Anyway, keep coming back. You'll notice the difference right away."

I suddenly feel better and leave for the locker room, able now to walk upright, with almost a bit of a bounce to my step. I look up at the mirror, and—wait a minute. Is there just the tiniest improvement in my stomach? Are my abs just a bit tighter? my thighs just a bit trimmer? my legs just a bit longer?

I pass the registration desk and decide to sign up for tomorrow's class.

Whoo-oo-oo-oo!

"It's Only a
Two-Hour Flight"

▲ . ■ . ▲ . ■ .

It is moments before takeoff at Gate 29, Flight 4, nonstop to Milwaukee. Annie and Alex sit in their double umbrella stroller, alert and rigid with excitement. Like hounds on the scent of foxes, they somehow *know* this is going to be fun. Meanwhile, my husband and I—alert and rigid with fear—stand at the window, staring blankly out at the runway. This will be our first plane ride with our children.

I admit right off that we are more than a bit leery about taking them on a plane. Both kids have been described kindly by friends as "active." But the incentive for this trip is strong: Tomorrow is my high school reunion, my parents have offered their services as full-time babysitters, and my husband loves my home state of Wisconsin. Besides, he adds, it is only a two-hour flight. What could our children do in two hours?

ıı my mind, I go over my list of take-on items. One ,roller, to be folded on board. One infant car seat, to put Alex in once the plane is at cruising level. One large and incredibly heavy baby bag carrying the following items: diapers, diaper wipes, pacifier, baby blanket, two milk bottles, one box of raisins, a bag of chocolate-chip cookies, one Mickey-Mouse-Dresses-Himself doll, five strips of *Sesame Street* stickers, coloring book, crayons, and a tube of Desitin.

In the side pocket are a bottle and a toddler cup filled with apple juice. Experienced parents have advised us to give the kids something to drink during takeoff and landing—forcing them to swallow and take the pressure off their ears. My husband and I, having traveled often by plane before our children were born, remember entire flights vibrating with the blood-curdling screams of infants suffering from ear problems. We are determined to be prepared with our own children.

"Attention passengers," booms a voice at the gate. "We'd like to ask those passengers with children to board at this time."

"That's us," says my husband, and we gather our equipment and push the stroller toward the gate. The other passengers, already there, standing impatiently, step back to let us pass. Their faces register a variety of expressions ranging from horror to disgust to despair.

"Oh, perfect. Perfect," mutters a man in a blue suit, clutching a laptop word processor.

Just before we enter the aircraft, we stop the stroller while I unbuckle Alex and my husband unbuckles Annie. He hands Alex to me while he tries to fold the easy-to-fold double-umbrella stroller. Only it won't fold easily today. My husband tries again. He sees Annie's Gumby doll wedged between the seat and the wheel. Passengers are lining up close behind us as my husband struggles to pull out Gumby. The flight attendant disappears into the cockpit. My husband rips off Gumby's head.

"Gumby! Gumby! Gumby!" sobs my daughter. The stroller folds.

The flight attendant reappears to take the stroller and we stumble to seats 1B and 1C.

As I hold Alex in one arm and the car seat in the other, Alex begins to wet his already loose diaper.

Annie points to the stream running down my arm. "Pee-pee," she announces to the passengers as they go by.

The other passengers do not find my children adorable. They brush past in their immaculate suits and their pee-pee–free dresses to get to their seats. It occurs to me that I have finally become the very person I used to avoid on planes.

My husband has settled Annie in her seat and helps Alex into his. Finally the four of us are seated. We had requested these bulkhead seats months ago, and while officially we are required to hold our children in our laps during takeoff and landing, we are both betting that the seats next to us will remain empty for our children. How right we are. One man stops at seat 1A, double-checks his ticket, glances at Annie pasting stickers to the wall, then races back to the flight attendant.

"No, I don't mind the last seat. Not at all," he says as he strides toward the back of the plane.

Finally it is time for takeoff. My husband holds Alex,

the bottle of juice poised at his lips. I hold Annie with one hand, her toddler cup with the other. As the plane ascends, I wait until I feel the pressure on my ears.

"Now!" I scream over the roar of the engine. We shove bottle and cup in our childrens' mouths. Stunned, they swallow. They swallow again. Then they gulp and finally they spit up, their eyes watering and their faces beet-red. Their ears are fine but they almost choked to death on apple juice.

"Are we there yet?" moans my husband from across the aisle.

The next two hours pass by in a painful blur of activity. Time seems to have stopped. Annie, bored with the headless Gumby, flings him at the lady behind us. Dinner arrives while my husband changes Alex's diapers. Annie's crayons slide under her seat onto the floor two seats away, where I finally retrieve them. Alex spits up his stewed carrots while the flight attendant comes by with coffee.

"More wine, please," says my husband.

After dinner Annie discovers the window shade; it occupies her for a full ten minutes. She snaps it up. "Up!" she screams. She snaps it down. "Down!" she screams. This is repeated until I show her the ashtray.

At one point I glance over at a woman about my age in seat 3B. She is wearing a silk blouse and linen slacks. There is a snifter of brandy on her tray and she is delicately popping peanuts into her mouth as she pages through *Vogue*. I remember doing that on a plane—a long, long time ago.

Finally it is time to descend. My husband and I, old hands at this by now, administer juice into the mouths of our children until the plane lands.

"Welcome to Milwaukee," the flight attendant says on the loudspeaker. "The temperature is a warm eighty degrees. Please remain seated until the plane comes to a complete stop."

The four of us sit, crumpled in our seats, and wait until the other passengers leave. I look around at the damage. Bottles, the toddler cup, crayons, and coloring books are strewn on the floor around us. Used diapers fall out of the sick bags. The Mickey-Mouse-Dresses-Himself doll lies in a pool of apple juice. I look at our children. Annie, quiet at last, sucks her thumb and pages through her *Pat-the-Bunny* book. Alex snores peacefully with a grin on his face. I look at my husband. He has a Big Bird sticker stuck to his forehead and spit-up on his right shoulder.

Now that we have the plane to ourselves, the stroller works perfectly. My husband gathers the empty milk bottles and toys into the baby bag while I strap in the kids. As we pass the flight attendant, she smiles at us for the first time.

"Your kids did great," she remarks, stepping back to let the cleaning crew through.

We look at her, incredulous.

"Oh, I've seen worse, really," she says. "Yours are ready for a longer trip—like maybe Hawaii."

I watch the crew start to scrape the chocolate-chip cookies off seats 1B and 1C.

Maybe next year.

I Remember
Slow Dancing

▲ ▪ ● ▲ ● ▪ ●

*M*y husband and I went to a wedding reception recently. Along with the champagne and good cheer, I was really looking forward to the prospect of dancing. We were, after all, away from our kids for a few hours, both of us were dressed up, and there was a wonderful old-fashioned band playing live music. From our table I looked longingly at the dance floor where an elderly couple was waltzing. They floated together—faces composed and serene, smiling at one another as they moved—still obviously in love. I thought with a sigh that I wanted desperately to join them and looked around for my husband. I found him sitting with the other men, huddled together on one side of the hall talking about last night's hockey game. Forlorn, I went over to join the wives, who were glaring at their sedentary mates from the other side of the hall. At least I had company in my misery. There seemed to be only one man our age who actually liked to dance. He liked to Lindy and he liked to Twist and he liked to Stroll. Best of all, he liked to slow dance. He even dipped, we noticed. Occasionally his wife begged off from fatigue and told him to ask some of the marooned women whose husbands wouldn't budge. When he asked me, I swallowed my pride and accepted eagerly. Over his shoulder I glanced at my husband, hoping for a streak of jealousy to overcome him. Instead he waved cheerfully and went back to talking about the game—relieved, no doubt, to be let off the hook. As glad as I was to be dancing, I wanted to be dancing with my husband. Finally I walked over to him and hissed "You promised at least one dance!" Reluctantly my husband excused himself from his buddies and danced with me. He is, after all, a man of his word. But the music was wrong and the lights were wrong and the words he was whispering had nothing to do with seduction. "Think we left enough diapers for the sitter?" he asked, spinning me around the floor.

Maybe I'm being too hard on him. But to me, dancing is a lot more than a few agile twists and turns on a waxed floor. To me it is what separates the dull, married-with-children couch-potato couples from the romantic, passionate, forever-young, forever-in-love types I see on dance floors at weddings.

When I was growing up in Racine, Wisconsin, as I remember, slow dancing with a boy was just about the most provocative thrill there was.

Picture this: It is 1966 and I am in the tenth grade. The

gym has been decorated with crêpe paper and balloons and a new revolving light, compliments of the senior class. The boys stand on one side of the gym—slouched with heads bent—huddled together in groups of five or six while girls stand on the other side, playing with strands of hair and peering hopefully across the room. The band finishes the last chords of "Wipe Out" and goes right into the first strains of "In the Still of the Night" (an oldie-but-goodie even back in 1966, when oldies first became goodies). The lights dim and a hush falls on the crowd. "In the still, de do, de do, de do, of the ni-ght..." the lead singer croons softly. I exchange glances with my girlfriends: a Slow Dance. We watch the coolest boy in the senior class walk over to the coolest girl in the junior class and soon they are dancing cheek to cheek under the revolving light. The chaperones become alert and begin to walk through the area as other couples start to pair up.

The anticipation is unbearable. Will I be asked to dance, I wonder? Or will I have gone through the ritual of bubble bath, hair wash, creme rinse, hair set on orange-juice cans, and finally Heaven Scent cologne on all my pressure points—for naught?

Just when it seems hopeless, just when I feel doomed to stand, larger than life, alone in the gym, alone in eternity, a tall boy with a crooked grin—resplendent in his Beatle boots and narrow tie—taps me on the back. "Wanna dance?" he asks, and I melt into his arms. We sway to the music, heads on each other's shoulders and eyes closed in ecstasy for a whole four minutes. Pretty heady stuff in 1966.

It was ten years later, at a friend's wedding, that my husband and I first met—on a dance floor and to the tune of the same song, it turned out. And although I was older and wiser by then, the romance of the moment couldn't have been stronger. We danced for hours that night. In fact, a few years later on our own wedding day, my husband teased me that the only reason I married him was so I would have a permanent in-house dance partner. And it is true that in the beginning we danced quite a bit.

However, as we got older, my husband became less enthusiastic about dancing in public—he claimed dances were for meeting girls and he'd already met one—but at least we still danced occasionally—in private. By the time our daughter Annie was born, most of our dancing took place in our living room. As soon as I'd put Annie down in the bassinet in our bedroom, my husband would put a stack of oldies-but-goodies on the stereo—classic slow-dancing tunes like "Whiter Shade of Pale" and "You've Lost That Lovin' Feeling" and "When a Man Loves a Woman." We'd dim the lights and the magic would return—until Annie woke up for her ten-o'clock feeding.

To this day, I still love slow dancing with my husband. But after the birth of Alex last year, we find we have less and less time for just ourselves—less and less time to slow dance. And, of course, two toddlers have made us tired—too tired to dance, even in our living room. It's hard to be romantic, for example, when our son is throwing steamed beets at his sister and Annie is grinding watermelon seeds into the carpet and the background music is Mr. Rogers singing "It's a Beautiful Day in the Neighborhood."

As a matter of fact, we dance so rarely these days that I fear my husband may have forgotten how. Besides, hardly anyone our age goes dancing any more. Our generation— caught between the big-band sound of the forties and the disco beat of the seventies—has somehow lost out on the art itself. Ballroom dancing, especially, belongs to a life- style we rejected back in the late sixties and seventies. And now that *we* have embraced the establishment (many of us have returned to the suburbs and are raising families) we have lost some important pieces along the way. Slow dancing belongs to other generations, not ours. When we crave romance and gallantry, we slide an old Fred Astaire– Ginger Rogers video into the VCR and marvel at their magic and elegance. Like others before us, we too need to escape from the grim realities of adulthood into a world of romance once in a while. How sad that we seem to have lost that grand gesture of courtship just when we need it the most.

Still, romance is wonderfully unpredictable. On this rainy Monday at the end of a very bad day, as I wipe strained carrots off my son's pajamas with one hand and try to draw Piglet for my daughter in her Winnie the Pooh coloring book with the other, my husband appears in the kitchen carrying a transistor radio. He turns up the volume to a familiar oldie-but-goodie and grabs my sticky hand. "Wanna dance?" he asks and turns off the fluorescent light. Both our children start to giggle and clap their hands in glee. It will be years before this sort of behavior on their parents' part will embarrass them. He wraps my arm around his shoulder and in the dark, in our sweatshirts, as the rain pounds down and Annie and Alex hum along, we sway to the music: "In the still, de do, de do, de do, of the ni-ght..."

He hasn't forgotten after all.

▲ ● ■ ● ▲ ● ■ ● ▲ ● ■ ● ▲ ● ■ ● ▲ ● ■ ● ▲ ● ■ ● ▲ ● ■ ● ▲ ● ■ ● ▲ ● ■ ● ▲ ● ■

The Girls We
Used to Be

▲ ● ■ ● ▲ ● ■ ●

*M*y best friend Amanda, who has never had children, stretch marks, or spit-up on her shoulder, is coming for a visit this weekend. And while I always look forward to seeing her, I am also filled with apprehension at the thought of three days with someone who is not used to sharing the bathroom with two toddlers, a potty trainer, and a diaper pail. On her last visit a few months ago, for example, my two-year-old daughter insisted on watching my friend go peepers on the grown-up potty. Amanda happily complied, eager to prove she was a good sport with my children. I am the same good sport when I visit her at her office, where she is often interrupted by important phone calls.

Amanda and I go way back, as they say. We began our friendship at age eighteen with everything in common. We roomed together in college, waitressed part-time at the same pizzeria off-campus, and after graduation left our small Midwestern hometowns for big cities—she for Chicago, I for New York.

Fifteen years later, Amanda has a high-powered career and lives in an immaculate duplex off North Shore Drive, and I live with my husband and two kids in a messy tract colonial in the suburbs of Long Island.

We are both, I am sure, satisfied with our lot in life. In fact, if we had to do it over again, I know Amanda would choose her corner office and I would choose my often-chaotic family life. However, whenever Amanda comes for a visit, we each tend to overcompensate for the other's life-style. She tries to prove how competent she is with her nieces and nephews and I try to prove how knowledgable I am with the business world. She tells me how to raise my children and I tell her how to handle her secretary.

We've managed to stay close all these years—mainly through weekly hour-long phone calls and periodic visits. Amanda is the one I call for the important decisions in my life, like whether or not I should go back to work full-time and whether or not I should grow out my bangs. Over the years we've developed a vernacular and a reference system all our own—so conspicuous that someone listening would have a tough time following our conversation. During any kind of soul-searching talk with Amanda, I know she can be counted on to tell me the unvarnished truth, even if I sometimes would prefer not hearing it. After all, Amanda remembers the girl I used to be before I became the mother I am today. And I remember the girl she used to be before she became the executive she is today. As the years go by, we find we are each other's connection to our past, to our youth, even to our dreams—battered though they are by now.

Despite all this, I often get twinges of envy when she visits. From the minute she walks through the door, my children are star-struck. They stare up at her in awe. It's a rare sight for them to see a woman my age in full makeup wearing pantyhose in broad daylight. Amanda shamelessly dotes on my kids, bringing them an obscene array of gifts each time she comes. Naturally they worship her. She also never tires of spending time with them, and as I watch her snuggled up with one on each side, the three of them chuckling and gurgling like something out of *Little House on the Prairie*, I am filled with a mixture of jealousy and appreciation.

Then there's the matter of personal grooming. Let's face it. Amanda looks sleek and polished and Very Put Together. But after all, I reason with myself as I step on the scale, there is an order in Amanda's life which entitles her to quiet spa dinners of grilled scallops and endive after a tough day at the office while I eat leftover Jello Pops over the kitchen sink.

It seems that Amanda has more time than I do, too, although I know she works long hours and frequently travels on business. Still, her days include appointments for facials and manicures and leg waxings while mine include appointments for rubella shots and preschool registration and babysitter interviews. During low moments of self-pity, I wonder if life—that life—is passing me by.

And it only takes a glance into Amanda's cosmetic travel bag to see that I have not been keeping up with the world of beauty. Each time she visits she brings with her a new, state-of-the-art Skin Regimen ("a simple, thirty-minute morning program," she explains patiently) designed to bring back my youthful glow. Her cosmetic gifts to me sit unopened on my bathroom shelf next to the Baby Tylenol.

Just as Amanda makes me see the world I am missing, I know I inadvertently make her see what she is missing, too. Once, for example, on a Saturday morning when both kids were in bed with my husband and me and all of us were trying to remember the words to "Mocking Bird," Amanda walked by with her cosmetic bag—en route to the bathroom. Although she smiled at us, I saw a look of such raw hunger on her face that it made me wince. I saw a similar look during my son's baptism. Amanda, his god-mother, stood at the altar next to me, and while the priest trickled water over Alex's forehead, murmuring in Latin, Amanda and I exchanged a glance. Another moment in our history, it seemed to say. Later she said she sometimes feels like all the moments in history are mine, and that she is just the observer.

There are times when it is hard to stay best friends. I get jealous of her life and she gets jealous of mine and I worry that I will become an overweight household drudge who screams at her children in supermarkets and she worries that she will become a hardened spinster who will end up lonely and bitter, living with ten cats.

But we stay together and hang on. As we get older, we hold this old friendship in high esteem, realizing that for women with different life-styles, it is a rare commodity. We know in our hearts that it is better to be best friends with nothing in common than not to be best friends at all.

And so on this Friday morning I prepare for Amanda's arrival. I clean the guest room and I call the babysitter and I negotiate with my husband for time off with my friend. She and I will go shopping in the afternoon and giggle over clothes and pore over the cosmetics counter and complain about men in general. She will purchase a new breast-firming cream and I will purchase a new rectal thermometer. We'll compare notes on our daily life: She'll pretend to be interested in my son's cradle cap and I'll pretend to be interested in safe sex. We'll splurge on an expensive, leisurely dinner and come home late. While the rest of the house is asleep, we'll sit in the living room with a glass of wine and talk long into the night, our voices low.

And we'll remember the girls we used to be.

Perfect Children
I Have Known
and Loathed

$\mathcal{I}$t wasn't until I started taking our two children—
ages two and a half and one—on little outings with
other toddlers that I began to realize that there were
children in this world who were better-behaved, better-
dressed, softer-spoken and, in general, more perfect than
my own. This came as a surprise to me, since before I had
children, I seemed to notice only screaming, unruly brats
in restaurants, malls, and other public places. Now that I
have two of my own, I've been noticing only the well-
behaved ones, the quiet ones, the ones gurgling peacefully
in strollers or calmly staring at colorful mobiles while their
mothers smile serenely into space. I've tried to avoid them,
but perfect children seem to be cropping up everywhere
these days.

I spotted one at a children's birthday party recently. A

mother there was holding her newborn baby—a cherub-faced little boy, all soft and cuddly. The other children gathered around, taking turns stroking him. My toddler, Annie, looked on from a distance.

The birthday girl and Perfect Child, Melissa Sue—in her white organza dress and unscuffed patent leather Mary Janes, her neatly combed hair held back with a pink ribbon—gently patted the baby while she sang softly, "Rock-a-bye baby, in the tree top. . . ." The other mothers positively swooned. "Isn't she sweet?" they squealed.

The new mother turned to my daughter. "Come say hello to Baby Eric," she said.

Annie gave a wide grin and elbowed her way up to the baby. Leaning over, she tenderly kissed him on the cheek. Then, with all her might, she smacked him squarely on his forehead.

"HI BABY!" she screamed in delight as we dragged her away.

Mortified, I apologized profusely while Melissa Sue comforted the wounded Baby Eric.

"Annie hurt Baby," she announced to the group.

"It's okay, Melissa Sue," said Eric's mother, looking at my daughter out of the corner of her eye, pointedly at me. "Annie was just being friendly, right?"

I gritted my teeth. "Right," I agreed, my arm wrapped around Annie, who was straining to get another shot at Eric. It was pointless, I knew, to try to defend my daughter's intentions—to explain that she was not vicious, just overly enthusiastic.

Unfortunately, observing the Perfect Child in action

only makes me more aware of my own children's short-comings and more eager to apologize for them.

Take Perfect Jason, for example. Please. I run into him and his mother at the supermarket at least once a week. It is usually at a time when I have brought along one of my kids who, invariably, is having a bad day. Jason, on the other hand, does not have bad days. Every time I see him he is sitting properly in the cart's toddler seat, safety belt secured, hands resting on the bar, looking adorable in his sailor suit while his mother coolly compares ketchup prices. Nothing tempts this child: not the cookie aisle, not the dairy case stacked with yogurt, not even the candy racks dangling invitingly at the register.

My son, on the other hand, barely held in check in his cart, careens wildly from side to side as I race down the aisles. One hand lunges at the sanitary napkin display and the other flings my diaper coupons into the salad bar. By the time we get home I am ready for three days of bed rest.

Then there is Perfect Sandra, my neighbor's four-year-old. She is proof that the acorn does not fall far from the tree. Her mother is, quite simply, the cleanest woman I know. Her house sparkles with chemical disinfectants. Her basement floor is waxed, her off-white carpet is still off-white after five years, and she uses a toothbrush to scrub between the bathroom tiles. Naturally I refuse to invite her into my house. Her daughter will surely follow in her footsteps.

Last week, against my better judgment, I brought Annie there for a neighborhood mother-daughter luncheon. Annie seemed to be on her best behavior that day, and I was just beginning to relax over my chicken salad when Perfect Sandra announced in a clear voice:

"Mommy, Annie wiped a booger on the sofa." And sure enough, as all heads turned in the direction of the sofa, we saw the evidence as it lay in gooey splendor, stretched majestically across the chintz cushion.

"Booger," Annie repeated solemnly.

As Sandra stood there, pointing in triumph, my daughter smiled proudly at her side. I wasn't sure which I wanted to strangle first.

The stories are endless. At restaurants my husband and I watch perfect children using salad forks to eat their salad and dessert forks to eat their dessert while our children compete to see who can shove the most spaghetti up their noses. In church the perfect child in front of us folds her tiny hands in prayer while ours reach for the ribbons on her hat. In shoe stores perfect children are prodded into various pairs of shoes while our children say emphatically "No" and kick the salesman in the groin.

My children have been called everything from "rather spirited" to "willful" to "undisciplined" to "Have-you-tried-medication?" They will never be called perfect.

But my husband and I know better. We see them at times when, away from the public eye, they seem, if not perfect, at least loving and warm and enthusiastic. When, for example, Annie climbs into Alex's crib to teach him to jump up and down and we hear their squeals of joy, we know we are the lucky ones. We wouldn't change Annie's exuberance or Alex's curiosity for all the perfect children there are.

And, on this peaceful Saturday afternoon, while they both take naps, we can't resist peering into their bedroom and marveling at our good fortune. We see Annie—her arm thrown over her head, her long eyelashes drawing shadows over her cheeks, her upper lip stained with grape juice—and we see Alex, curled up into a ball, in rare repose, sprouts of brown hair shooting up straight and his fists clenched under his chin. We know we have only a couple of hours before they will wake up, recharged and eager to take on the rest of the day. Then my husband and I will put down our newspapers and rinse out our coffee cups and march upstairs to greet our imperfect children. We can hardly wait.

A Weekend
Alone

FRIDAY

*M*aybe this wasn't such a good idea after all, I think as we drive to the airport. When my husband offered me a weekend at my sister's as part of my birthday present, I had hesitated. After all, I had never left the children for more than a few hours, much less overnight. Besides, Alex was still teething and Annie was at that stage when being away from me—if only briefly—induced unbridled panic. What decent mother would go off on a vacation without her kids? But my husband pointed out that seventy-two hours was hardly a vacation. It was, he insisted, more like a rest, and we both agreed that I needed a rest. Well into my thirties, motherhood had come late for me and, compounded by a part-time job, two births in eighteen months had left me... well, tired. The very prospect of a decent night's sleep made me giddy. This would give my husband a chance to bond with his children. I'd practically be doing him a favor. I said yes.

Now I'm having second thoughts. I peek into the rearview mirror and notice Annie, sucking her thumb and eyeing me suspiciously. She knows something is up. Alex chews on his car-seat strap and smears the window with a soggy biscuit. I glance at my husband staring grimly in front of him, lost in thought, both hands on the steering wheel.

I begin to go over, for the third time, my list of helpful hints—what to give Alex for breakfast, what kind of barrettes Annie insists on wearing, what nighttime books to read to which child, where to find the extra supplies of diapers, vitamins, undershirts, baby shampoo. I drone on endlessly.

Before I know it, we are at the airport. As we had planned earlier, I kiss everyone goodbye and leave quickly before the kids figure out that I'm gone.

Inside the plane, I force myself to relax. I watch a young mother board with two small children. She is wearing what I usually wear, the uniform of motherhood: loose top, sweat pants, and sneakers. Her face is flushed as she tries to settle her children into their seats and fumbles through a plastic bag for their toys. My heart reels with empathy as I remember my first plane ride with my own children. Now I sit alone in my window seat, all dressed up in my "without-children" clothes— with new matching handbag. I unlatch the clasp and pull out several snapshots of Annie and Alex that I have promised to bring to my sister. My children grin up at me from their kiddie pool in our backyard, from their high-chairs in the kitchen, from the merry-go-round at our neighborhood park.

SATURDAY MORNING

I awaken on my sister's sofabed. It is 6:00 A.M. I remember drifting off to sleep around 11:00 P.M. after a peaceful lasagna dinner and several hours of "catch-up" talk with my sister while we sat in our pajamas in her living room. I count on my hand: I have been unconscious for seven hours! I feel confused, disoriented, like a patient waking from a prolonged coma. Where am I? I mutter. And why is it so quiet? Then I remember. I pull my sister's white comforter to my chin and survey her sleek apartment. It is filled with all the accoutrements of a childless life-style—glass cocktail table with sharp corners, pastel Oriental rug, crystal vase filled with fresh flowers, and in the hall two uncapped electrical outlets. Through her windows I can see the swimming pool and tennis courts. My sister, eager to make my stay restful and stress-free, has organized the day: morning tennis, afternoon pool, evening dinner where we'll be joined by my old college roommate-and-still-best-friend Amanda, and possibly a stop at the newest chic nightspot. I make coffee and bring it back to my sofabed. It is too early for anyone without children to be up.

I picture my husband in the frantic early morning hours at home—Annie will be in her highchair trying to feed herself Cheerios, and Alex will be drooling in his infant seat. Cartoons will be blaring on the TV and the morning will seem to last forever. My husband will probably not be in the best of moods. I decide not to call. Besides, he had advised me not to call home unless there was an emergency; instead I should try to enjoy my newfound freedom. He is right. I return to the kitchen and pour myself a second cup of coffee.

SATURDAY AFTERNOON

My sister and I lie by the pool. She reads a novel while I gape at the stream of young, well-toned singles surrounding us on nearby chaises. The sheer luxury of having this much free time amazes me. I shamelessly eavesdrop on conversations, feeling for the moment like an alien landed from Jupiter. The women discuss men and their jobs and the men discuss sports and their jobs. The men have muscled shoulders and recent haircuts. The women have tanned thighs and flat stomachs; they wear high-cut bikinis in neon greens and pinks. I am wearing a conservative black one-piece. It has one of those new tummy control panels. I begin to feel sorry for myself until my sister asks to see photos of my children. Again I take out the snapshots of Annie and Alex and I watch my sister's face grow soft as she stares at each picture intently. I look at them over her shoulder and feel better. Nevertheless, I suck in my stomach as I walk to the soda machine.

SATURDAY NIGHT

After a delicious dinner with my sister and Amanda, I agree to a nightcap at the aforementioned chic nightspot. The cover charge alone is enough to keep my children in diapers for a week. We are seated in a dark burgundy velvet booth, listening to a serious jazz combo playing in the corner. I am wearing an elegant silk dress of my sister's, pantyhose, and high heels. The last time I had been out this late was to run to the all-night pharmacy for an infant nasal syringe.

Three men approach us. They smile at the three of us. We smile back. They begin to chat. Have you been here before? Where do you live? How do you like the jazz combo? It is apparent they are eager to get to know us. Overcome by the spirit of friendship and the spontaneity of the moment, I take out the photographs of Annie and Alex.

"This was last Christmas. Oh, and here's my husband changing Alex's diaper for the first time." I point to another: "You can actually see Annie smiling if you look closely—well, maybe it's too dark in here..." My voice trails off as I become aware of a sudden silence, a coolness in the mood. The three men begin backing away.

"You must be very proud," one of them murmurs kindly as they disappear into the crowd. My sister and best friend exchange glances.

"Time to call it a night?" my sister asks.

SUNDAY EVENING

On the plane going home—my last precious hour of freedom—I indulge in a glass of white wine and reflect on the high points of my trip: the long, uninterrupted bubble bath, the aimless shopping and sampling at cosmetic counters, the hours of catching up with my sister and my friend. These were luxuries I'd be doing without for quite a while. Being a mother meant never having any time, I conclude as the plane begins its descent. By the time the plane lands, however, my thoughts turn to home. I begin to wonder how they have survived his weekend. Will Annie sulk when she sees me? Did Alex get his tooth yet? Will my husband speak to me?

As I walk toward the gate, I can already see the three of them, although they do not yet see me. Annie is wearing a mismatched overall set and is rhythmically kicking at Alex's stroller. Her hair, I am sure, has not been combed since Friday. Alex, slumped in his stroller, is missing a shoe and gurgles at his sister. My husband has a two-day beard and looks tired. Still, he picks up Alex to kiss him and says something to Annie. Then I hear Annie's giggle and suddenly my heart leaps and knocks with a thud. There is my family, standing together among the throngs of strangers, waiting to take me home—where I belong. I break into a run.

We Never Argued
Until We Had
Children

The first couple of years my husband and I were married we hardly ever argued. After all, we had no children then, so what was there to argue about? Oh, there were mild disagreements concerning the color of the wallpaper or the choice of microwave, but nothing serious. Nothing compared to the knock-down, drag-out fights we have now over important issues like whose turn it is to put the teething gel on Alex's gums at three in the morning or who left the port-o-crib out in the rain the previous night.

Once you have children your pattern of fighting changes, and then of course the rules of fighting also change. You find there's a whole new world out there to argue about. We now fight about how long one of us gets to read the Sunday papers while the other one makes breakfast for the kids at 5:45 A.M. We fight about the amount of sweets they should have and whether we should let them cry in their rooms and who has to pick up the babysitter. But most of all we fight over the actual time each of us must spend watching them.

In the beginning I was a pushover. I watched the kids all the time since my husband seemed to usually have very important reasons for going to the hardware store or working on the car. It took me a while to figure out that I was doing more custodial care than he was.

Since both my husband and I work full time, I feel it is only fair to divide the child care right down the middle. After all, we had always divided up household chores as well as household expenditures pretty evenly. My husband had always appreciated my fair-mindedness in this area; even when we dated years ago I insisted on paying for my half most of the time. And so naturally when we had children I figured we'd just continue along in the same way. But now I know that once you have children, your husband reverts back to the previous century in his attitudes about raising children. Suddenly, "a child needs his mother" is the refrain he offers at three in the morning and in the middle of the dinner party you are giving. My husband loves to do the fun stuff with the kids—buying ice-cream cones and going to a parade and teaching them how to swim—but changing diapers and giving baths and doling out baby medicine are just *too confusing* for a man to figure out.

I am happy to report, however, that I have since learned the ropes a bit and can pretty much hold my own against my husband when it comes to deciding who does what.

This was not accomplished without breaking some dishes, so to speak, and it is a triumph that is constantly being challenged. I do have a few tricks up my sleeve, though, which I am happy to share with my sisters in need. Here is a typical scenario:

The Family Room on a
Rainy Saturday Afternoon in March

There is no babysitter in sight for the entire weekend and, in the words of your kids, there is nothing to do. Both toddlers are aimlessly wandering around the room, their noses running. One is humming and the other one is whining. The entrance is blocked off by a gate. Your husband is sitting there next to you, leafing through last week's *Sports Illustrated*, his eyes darting back and forth like a caged animal's. The VCR is broken and you are out of animal crackers. What is a mother to do? I offer several escape hatches—all within easy access from the family room:

1. *The bathroom.* Suddenly double over with stomach cramps. Ask if there's any Motrin in the house. What can your husband do except open the gate and let you hobble into the upstairs bathroom where you have stashed this week's *People* magazine and a Diet Coke. Escape time: twenty minutes.

2. *The telephone.* Have a friend call you, disguising her voice as the preschool teacher. Look frantically at

your husband and tell him to get the preschool file, quick. Then tell him you have to take the call UP-STAIRS, where it is quiet. Go upstairs to the bedroom, lie down, and chat with your friend. Hear how her trip to St. Croix went. Or hang up and just lie there and listen to the silence. Escape time: thirty minutes.

3. *The laundry room* (stay with me). Peel off a few dirty pieces of the children's clothes, and say you have to put in a quick load along with the shirts your husband will need on Monday. Go down to the basement, throw them quickly into the washer, then unfold a lawn chair and browse through your high school yearbooks, which have been gathering mildew there for years. Just before you go upstairs, start the washer, leaving the basement door open as proof of your chore. Then return to the family room, warning your husband that the washer is really acting up. Escape time: forty minutes.

Of course, all this isn't to say your husband won't try to get even—in his own way. My husband, naturally, has found his own formulas for revenge and uses a variety of methods that he knows will drive me crazy.

For example, my husband knows full well that I have an aversion to dirty diapers. Whenever I have to change a diaper I hold my breath, retaping it tight, then immediately throw it out. But my husband, whenever he changes Alex's diaper, leaves it just sitting there, open. He leaves used diapers all over, never—not once!—putting them in the diaper pail even though it is often ONLY TWO FEET AWAY! Instead it sits there—on the changing table or the dining-room table or on our bed—open in all its glory. The Desitin is usually left uncapped also so that Annie can have something to play with on the new sofa. I have finally figured out why he does this. He does it to prove he actually changed a diaper and likes to keep the evidence right in plain sight.

He has his own ways of escaping his kids, too. He has gotten in the habit, for example, of taking thirty-minute baths; *before* we had children his five-minute showers were legendary. The garage, always such a mess that it was impossible to park a bicycle, much less a car, is now incredibly clean and neat—due, of course, to my husband's feverish care on Saturday mornings and whenever Alex is getting new teeth. And whenever we have company these days, my husband insists on making drinks and cooking dinner, leaving me with one kid on my lap and the other helping herself to the jalapeño dip.

Now that we have children, we sometimes chuckle—in rare moments of quiet, once we put the kids in bed—over all the silly things we used to spend hours quibbling about late at night at the kitchen table: things like the fuel bill and refinancing our home mortgage and what kind of car to get and when our CDs would mature.

Now we don't sweat the small stuff.

"Mommie and Me"

▲•■•▲•■•

I am in a good mood this morning as I drive Annie to the first session of "Mommie and Me," a library program designed for toddlers and their mothers who want to spend quality time together. Annie will love the reading and coloring part, I am sure, and I am confident she will be the star pupil at our library. Besides, she really needs the attention these days. When Alex was born last year, Annie went from being the only child to being the older child, and that, combined with my returning to the work force a few months ago, has made me begin to feel guilty about not spending enough time with her.

Naturally, I am feeling quite pleased with myself for planning these outings and figure I have everything under control. After some maneuvering, I can manage to take off a couple of hours from work every Tuesday during my lunch hour. I calculate fifteen minutes to get home and then pick up Annie, leave Alex with our babysitter, drive to the library. After the program, drive Annie back home, drive myself back to work. Eat a yogurt at my desk. Couldn't be easier.

I can, in fact, actually feel the guilt melting off my shoulders as I pull into the parking lot this cool and crisp autumn day. As we get out of the car, Annie sees her favorite park, which is right next to the library.

"Park!" Annie says in delight, as she races over to the playground.

"No, not today!" I shout, running after her. But she is already on the merry-go-round, her arms and legs wrapped around the bars.

"Today's SPECIAL!" I grunt, dragging her away. "And we don't want to be late, do we?"

Annie's face begins to crumple, and she revs up to a high-decibel shriek just as we enter the library. We follow the chipmunk signs downstairs to the children's department.

Sitting in a circle by the window are nine well-behaved toddlers. Their mothers sit behind them chatting quietly with one another until I bring in Annie, whose shrieking has become a low-pitched howl.

Annie takes one look at the group.

"No-o-o-o-o-o," she sobs, leaning against me and refusing to join the circle.

A tiny woman in a powder-blue corduroy jumper appears.

"I'm Miss Margaret," she tells the circle of children in a singsong voice. "And welcome to the 'Mommie and Me' program." She turns abruptly toward Annie and me as we stand uncertainly near the bookshelves.

"Please-take-a-seat-you're-disturbing-the-other-children," she says through gritted teeth. Looking up brightly at the class, she continues. "Can we all say 'Mommie and me'?"

"Mommie and me!" chirp the children.

"Say 'Mommie and me,' Honey," I plead with Annie.

Annie clamps her lips tight in defiance.

"Here's a nametag for each of you," says Miss Margaret. "And Mommies, your nametags match your child's forest creature!" Annie's and mine resemble ferrets. Miss Margaret assures me they are woodland badgers. My daughter rips hers in half anyway. Miss Margaret takes a seat on a tiny stool and holds up a songbook.

"Does everyone here know the Bus Song?" All heads nod except for Annie's. My heart sinks. She doesn't know the Bus Song because her mother didn't teach it to her! Her mother was too busy fulfilling her own needs by working Outside the Home during the day and watching Oprah Winfrey while she cooks dinner.

The song has started and the children sway to and fro to the rhythm of the words. They make hand gestures with each new verse; Annie looks on in dismay—an orphan with her nose pressed against the bakery window.

The hour drags on interminably. After reading several stories, Miss Margaret chooses one my daughter recognizes. We have the same book at home and have spent many happy hours reading it together; for a moment I swell with pride. See, I look at the other mothers, I DO read to my children. But when Annie sees the book she leaps up to grab it.

"Mine!" she says, and takes it out of Miss Margaret's hand. But Miss Margaret, who wasn't born yesterday, grabs it back.

"What do we do with this book, boys and girls?" she asks, holding it high above her head.

"SHARE!" they scream back in triumph.

Annie is so stunned by the outburst that she sits, subdued for the time being, and listens.

After story time it is time to color. Miss Margaret gives each toddler a piece of paper and tells them to sit at the big round table.

Everyone takes a place except Annie, who has noticed the card catalogue. Systematically she pulls out each drawer until it crashes to the floor.

Well, this is the last straw for me. I grab Annie, put back each drawer, and leave the children's department. Miss Margaret looks visibly relieved. The alarm sounds as we open the door, and the security guard, who had been reading *Popular Mechanics* in the corner, comes running over.

My daughter is holding on to the Bus Songbook. We are going to learn that song, I vow, if it kills me. I check out the book and we go directly home.

"How'd it go?" asks our sitter.

"Just great," I lie, and hand over Annie, who seems just as happy to be home as I am. I change my clothes and drive back to work.

Sitting at my desk and waiting for my respiration to return to normal, I dwell on Annie and our morning together. "Mommie and Me" had not gone well, I admit as I open my yogurt. How could Annie have been so obnoxious? I was so sure she'd be thrilled to spend some time with me. Where had I failed? Was it because I went back to work? I remind myself that although my own mother never worked I still managed to grow up with more than my share of neurotic tendencies.

To make matters worse, I must return to work after dinner tonight for a meeting and won't even be able to do my usual bedtime routine with Annie.

By six o'clock that evening I am standing in the bathroom trying to apply mascara. Annie is standing beside me, watching intently. I have tried to shoo her downstairs with my husband, who is feeding Alex, but Annie is determined to stay here. She keeps reaching for my makeup bag, and in desperation I hand her an empty compact with a brush. She watches me brush on the blush, then carefully brushes it on herself. After I apply lipstick, I bend over and put on some lip gloss on her lips. She squeals happily.

I smile in spite of myself, and for the next few moments we apply our makeup side by side in compatible silence—I in my bathrobe and Annie in her undershirt.

Suddenly she looks up at me, pokes a finger in my stomach, and smiles.

"Mommie and me," she says contentedly, and then points to herself.

I knew she'd get it right.

Dining at Home
with the Family

▲●■●▲●■●

I sometimes hate going to the pediatrician with my children because inevitably he hits me with some piece of advice or information that makes me feel even more insecure as a parent than I did before I walked through the doors.

The last time I went there, for example, he gave me this brochure on the importance of eating with your toddlers: "Mealtime Suggestions That Can Be Given to Parents at the 18-Month Health Supervision Visit." This hit a sore spot with my husband and me, since we haven't had much luck in that area. In fact, we were getting into the habit of planting both kids in front of the TV with their dinner while we sat in the living room and actually had a conversation. It had been working out pretty well, but I knew in the back of my mind it was not what a good parent would do.

I would also run into other mothers in the waiting room who would brag about their family meals and how warm and wonderful they were. They obviously didn't need the brochure.

"We even include the baby at dinner," said one woman smugly. "All five of us sit at the dining room table and discuss the day's events. It's just my favorite time of the day!"

I looked at her closely. She's got to be lying, I think to myself. Or on some new tranquilizer in time-release capsule form. On the other hand, I shouldn't draw conclusions without proof.

And so tonight is the night we are all going to dine as a family. My husband is supportive in this endeavor, envisioning future traditional meals where he sits at the head of the table and presides over his charges—his wife deferring to his judgment and setting a good example for his children. In his enthusiasm, he has volunteered to make one of his special dishes and is at this minute putting the finishing touches on the ratatouille. The salad has been crisped, and the bread is warm. I glance down at the pediatrician's xeroxed brochure propped up in my plexiglass cookbook stand. I read aloud to my husband:

The following guidelines will help you teach appropriate mealtime behavior. You and your child will enjoy mealtime and will be able to look forward to it as a special time you have together.

"You're sure this is going to work?" asks my husband.
I continue:

Guidelines for Improving Mealtime Behavior:

1. Turn off the television.
I go into the family room where Annie and Alex sit, mesmerized by Bambi's mother, who is about to buy the farm. I turn off the TV just as the shot rings out and say brightly "Tonight we are all going to eat together in the dining room!" Annie, at three, is an excellent negotiator. She walks behind me and turns on the TV.

"No, Mom," she says patiently.

My husband, at this point, comes into the room and scoops up both kids and brings them, howling, into the dining room. He straps Alex into the highchair and Annie into the booster seat.

2. Set a reasonable time limit—25 minutes—for the meal. You may set a kitchen timer to indicate when the meal is over.
My husband sets the timer for ten minutes. "Compromise?" he shouts over the screaming.

3. Establish mealtime rules. Some examples are: (1) Remain seated. (2) Use silverware, not your hands. (3) Don't throw food. (4) Close your mouth when you chew.
I bring in the ratatouille, salad, and bread. I dish out portions in the children's dishes as Annie and Alex watch in stunned silence.

"E–yew!" Annie says, holding her nose in disgust.

"Hmmmmm, good!" I say. "This is Daddy's special food! Much better than old peanut butter sandwiches!"

"No, no, no, no!" Annie chants and slides off her chair, backing into the corner.

Alex, ever the independent thinker, picks up some eggplant and tastes it. He makes a face, pulls it out of his mouth, and hurls it at the wall, where it stays. In finale, he picks up his dish and dumps it on Annie's plate.

"Kooties!" she shrieks and smacks it off the table, where it lands on our Oriental rug.

My husband pours us each a glass of wine. Annie walks over to him and asks, "What's that, Daddy?"

"Mommie and Daddy's juice, Honey. Now go sit down." He looks up at me. "Bring some peanut butter. I'll make them sandwiches."

3. Include your children in the conversation. Do not nag, threaten, or shout. Talk about things you know will interest them.

The children have calmed down a bit. They eat their sandwiches and idly bang their forks on their plates. I take a deep breath.

"What did you do in nursery school today, Annie?"

"I wanna watch Bambi."

"Did you learn any new songs?"

"Bambi, Bambi, Bambi," says Alex tearfully.

"Pass the wine," I say.

4. Praise your child frequently for appropriate behavior. You cannot praise too often.

"What the hell do you think you're doing?" yells my husband. I look up to see Alex unscrewing the cap of the salad dressing. I grab the bottle and place it in the middle of the table.

"Alex is a BAD boy, huh, Mommie?"

"Be quiet and quit kicking the table."

5. Do not give your child dessert, snacks, or drinks if your child does not finish dinner. Do not allow your child to eat or drink anything except water until the next meal.

The children have eaten half their sandwiches and none of their salad. They are both getting antsy. Although neither my husband nor I has eaten much of the ratatouille, we have made quite a dent in the Chianti. Alex has begun his famous whine, rising to an incredible pitch, which he's able to sustain indefinitely. Annie is using her fork to stab the bread.

My husband looks at me pointedly. "Will you give them something to shut them up?" he says under his breath.

"Like what? You know I don't like to give them sugar."

My husband jumps up and goes to the kitchen, returning a moment later with cookies and icepops. Annie and Alex break into smiles and for a while there is peace as the kids rot out their teeth and my husband and I finish off the wine.

The timer goes off, jarring us all from our reverie.

My husband sighs. "Okay, Annie, you can go watch Bambi now."

Annie and Alex grin at one another.

"Wanna stay," Annie declares cheerfully.

Can't wait until breakfast.

Happy Endings

▲●■●▲●■●

*M*y mother's favorite movie is *The Sound of Music,* mainly because it has a happy ending: Julie Andrews marries the man of her dreams and the seven children get a mom. She plays an ex-nun—a realistic touch because you'd have to be extremely religious to take on some man's seven children. Anyway, my mother won't go to a movie that doesn't have a happy ending, nor will she read novels with particularly depressing topics. "Why should I spend good money to see death, poverty, illness, and divorce? That I can get from reading the newspapers!" she says emphatically.

I admit that kind of attitude used to irritate me when I was in college and wanted to have deep discussions on intellectual movies like *One Flew over the Cuckoo's Nest* and *Dog Day Afternoon.* But she refused, instead going with my father to see *The Sunshine Boys* and *Cactus Flower*.

She did join my sister and me at *Terms of Endearment*, though, thinking it was a mother–daughter comedy, but almost walked out when Debra Winger got sick. And it took a lot of persuasion to get her to see *On Golden Pond* a few years later because she couldn't stand the thought of Katharine Hepburn and Henry Fonda as senior citizens. We talked about it a bit afterward at a diner, but she ended up changing the subject (as she often does) by saying "Let's talk about something more cheerful!" (This is the same woman who has often advised me to scrub the kitchen floor as a method of "curing the blues"). I used to think her whole attitude was—while not simple-minded, at least a rose-colored view of life. And I couldn't understand why my mother, a woman of great intelligence and depth, would deliberately avoid those films of such consequence. I wrote it off finally—figuring that, like many of my friends' mothers, it was a throwback to her Depression youth when everyone went to the movies to escape reality.

Now I know better. Now I know that it's because she is a mother, and mothers know instinctively that danger and tragedy lurk behind every corner, that their children are never really completely safe—not even when their parents do everything humanly possible to protect them. Therefore, in order to get through the day, mothers need to believe in happy endings. And now that I have children of my own, I find I'm beginning to recognize that same need in myself.

Last month, for example, Annie fell down on our cement patio and had eight stitches taken in her forehead at our local emergency room. That night she had a nightmare, shrieking out around 4:00 A.M. I jumped up and ran into her room.

"Bad dream, Mommie," she whimpered, and for a long time I sat with her, stroking her forehead, until she went back to sleep (I knew that's what she wanted me to do because that's what my mother had done for me when I was Annie's age and I woke up with a nightmare). I began to wonder—sometime before dawn—how my mother had managed to survive childrearing for all those years. As I looked down at my daughter's stitches, a kaleidoscope of possible future tragedies whirled through my mind—car accidents and kidnappings and terminal illness and drownings and child abuse. It is, I suppose, the price we pay for loving our children.

And suddenly all the memories I have of my mother began to take on a different meaning, too. Surely the stories my father told whenever we looked through old photographs proved that she, in her early years as a new parent, had to face the grimmer aspects of life—certainly to a larger degree than I ever have had to. I remember that when she was about my age she attended a funeral of her friend's daughter, who died of polio at age five. Apparently the little girl and I had gone to dancing school together. I've seen grainy snapshots of the two of us in our tap shoes, our mothers standing proudly behind us.

And yet I don't recall my mother showing any sadness at any time during my childhood—I remember only giggling with her during our shopping days at Gimbel's and the family picnics on the shores of Lake Michigan and her bridge club meeting in the living room, where the sound of laughter rang out long into the night throughout the 1960s.

Last year she watched her best friend—of over forty years—die of cancer. And what did these two old friends do in the last few months, when Chris still had some strength left? Did they discuss death and dying and leaving your husband and grandchildren? No, my mother admitted afterward, they never actually went into that in any detail. Instead my mother went over to Chris's house one afternoon and together they cleaned out her bathroom linen closet. The closest they got to touching on the topic was when Chris told my mother that she worried that her husband would never be able to find a *thing* if she didn't straighten out some of these sheets and towels—and she asked my mother to get something only she could reach on the highest shelves.

And so, as the years go on, my mother has become even more genial and light-hearted. In our weekly phone conversations she always changes the subject if we get too near any topic too depressing. She loves to hear about the children, and no matter how much I complain about Annie's sleepless nights or Alex's refusal to go peepers in the pottie, my mother always laughs and says "These are the best years of your life—enjoy them!" And I always hang up the phone and repeat her comment to my husband, who is usually changing a diaper or scraping squashed peas off the carpet. And he always answers "If these are the best years of our lives, God help us when the kids start school." I am not fooled, of course. It is just my mother being cheerful.

Now that I understand her better, I find myself becoming more like my mother each day. I tend to watch movies with happier endings than I did in the past—the last unsettling film I saw was *A Cry in the Dark*, and I didn't sleep for a week—Meryl Streep's baby in the crocheted bonnet was burned into my memory. I too am learning the grimmer aspects of life. Now that I have two children, I find I am so terrified of losing them that I can't even read the front page of the newspapers any more or watch the evening news. In the past I had a morbid fascination with murder stories and read each horrific newspaper article with eagerness. These days, however, whenever the television news even touches upon child abuse or the infant mortality rate or crack-addicted babies, I find myself groping frantically for the remote control and switching to *Entertainment Tonight*, where I try to become engrossed in the latest celebrity weight loss.

At any rate, when my mother comes for a visit these days, I know what to do. I no longer mind my mother discussing the geraniums and the impatiens instead of the environment—or the children's shoe sizes instead of their emotional development—or her neighbor's new retirement home instead of life expectancy in widows.

I just lean back and listen, enjoying her company and feeling grateful for our time together. Then after I put the children to bed, I slide *The Sound of Music* video into the VCR, hand my mom some popcorn, and sing along with Julie.

We both want to believe in happy endings.